TEACHING LEARNING DISABLED STUDENTS AT THE SECONDARY SCHOOL LEVEL

Naomi Zigmond • Janet Sansone
Sandra E. Miller
Kathleen A. Donahoe • Rachel Kohnke

*What
Research
and
Experience
Say to
the Teacher
of
Exceptional
Children*

The Council for Exceptional Children

Library of Congress Cataloging-in-Publication Data
Main entry under title:

Teaching learning disabled students at the secondary school level.

   (What research and experience say to the teacher of exceptional chil-
dren)
   "A product of the ERIC Clearinghouse on Handicapped and Gifted
Children."
   Bibliography: p. 45
1. Learning disabled children—Education (Secondary)—United States.
2. Resource programs (Education) 3. Classroom environment—United
States. 4. Lesson planning—United States. I. Zigmond, Naomi, 1941–. II.
Council for Exceptional Children. III. ERIC Clearinghouse on Handi-
capped and Gifted Children.

IV. Series.
LC4705.T32   1986   371.92   85-27990
ISBN 0-86586-161-7

A product of the ERIC Clearinghouse on Handicapped and Gifted Children.

Published in 1986 by The Council for Exceptional Children, 1920 Association Drive, Reston, Virginia 22091–1589.

Work on this monograph was supported by funds from the Handicapped
Personnel Preparation branch of Special Education Programs through grant
#G008301637, Special Project: A Teacher Center Experience for Secondary
Special Education Teachers.

This publication was prepared with funding from the U.S. Department of
Education, Office of the Assistant Secretary for Educational Research and
Improvement, contract no. 400-84-0010. Contractors undertaking such projects under government sponsorship are encouraged to express freely their
judgment in professional and technical matters. Prior to publication the
manuscript was submitted to The Council for Exceptional Children for critical review and determination of professional competence. This publication
has met such standards. Points of view, however, do not necessarily represent the official view or opinions of either The Council for Exceptional
Children or the Department of Education.

Printed in the United States of America.

Contents

About the Authors   v

1   Designing a Program for the Learning Disabled Adolescent   1

2   Planning for Instruction   13

3   Organizing Instruction to Maximize Student Learning   29

4   Beyond Direct Services for the Learning Disabled Adolescent   37

5   Recommendations for the Learning Disabilities Teacher   41

References   45

What Research and Experience Say to the Teacher of Exceptional Children

Series Editor: June B. Jordan

Series Editorial Committee: Carolyn M. Callahan, Herbert T. Goldstein, Alice H. Hayden, Merle B. Karnes, Thomas C. Lovitt, Joseph S. Renzulli

Other published titles in the Series:

- Managing Inappropriate Behaviors in the Classroom
  Thomas C. Lovitt

- Developing Creativity in the Gifted and Talented (out of print)
  Carolyn M. Callahan

- Early Childhood
  Merle B. Karnes and Richard C. Lee

- Social Environment of the Schools
  Maynard C. Reynolds, Editor

- Reasoning Abilities of Mildly Retarded Learners
  Herbert T. Goldstein and Marjorie T. Goldstein

- Affective Education for Special Children and Youth
  William C. Morse, John Ardizzone, Cathleen Macdonald, and Patricia Pasick

- Cross Age and Peer Tutoring: Help for Children with Learning Problems
  Joseph R. Jenkins and Linda M. Jenkins

About the Authors

Naomi Zigmond is Professor of Special Education at the University of Pittsburgh and Senior Scientist at the Learning Research and Development Center. She received her Doctorate from Northwestern University after majoring in language pathology and learning disabilities. Dr. Zigmond has served as a language pathologist at the Child Development Laboratory of Massachusetts General Hospital, as an instructor in the Harvard Medical School, and as an Assistant Professor at Boston University. She directed the Learning Center at Northwestern University and Psychoeducational Clinic at Boston University. In 1970, Dr. Zigmond joined the faculty at the University of Pittsburgh, with teaching responsibilities primarily in the area of assessment and remediation. Since 1975, Dr. Zigmond has been actively involved in research in special education, primarily at the secondary level. She served as director of a Child Service Demonstration Center for Urban Secondary Students with Learning Disabilities. She is currently codirector of a curriculum development study of School Survival Skills for secondary school-age students and director of a follow-up study of LD graduates and dropouts from the Pittsburgh Public Schools. Dr. Zigmond has written extensively about her work with LD students and on issues related to program planning, evaluation, and mainstreaming of secondary school-age mildly handicapped students.

Janet Sansone is a Research Assistant Professor of Special Education at the University of Pittsburgh. Dr. Sansone has a long history of consultation with secondary public school programs, most notably in the Pittsburgh Public School district. She served for 4 years in the Pittsburgh Public Schools as a full-time consultant to secondary mainstream teachers at one of the sites of a Child Service Demonstration Center for urban secondary students with learning disabilities. Dr. Sansone has coordinated several federally funded University of Pittsburgh special education projects, among them, an inservice training program for teacher consultants in middle and secondary schools, a mixed-category program for teachers of mildly handicapped students, and a Teacher Center training program for secondary special education teachers. Prior to her work in Pittsburgh, she served for several years as a teacher of secondary mainstream students, LD students, and SED students, both in public and private schools in the Ann Arbor, Michigan area. Currently Dr. Sansone is director of a Master's level Special Education training program preparing teachers of mentally and physically handicapped students. Her research interests include the study of mainstreaming procedures, the impact of secondary school contexts on LD students, and effective teaching practices.

Sandra E. Miller is a doctoral student in Educational Psychology at the University of Pittsburgh. She has taught elementary, middle school, and high school students and served as a residential counselor for American high school students living in Mallorca, Spain. For the past several years, Ms. Miller has collaborated in the design of a classroom observation instrument and coordinated an evaluation study of the impact of an inservice training program for secondary school teachers in the Pittsburgh Public Schools.

Kathleen A. Donahoe is a doctoral student in the Special Education Department at the University of Pittsburgh. She earned her Master's degree in Special Education at Indiana University of Pennsylvania. She has taught students with various exceptionalities at the secondary level for 8 years. She is currently involved in an intensive inservice endeavor which is designed to retrain and rejuvenate secondary educators of mildly handicapped students. Her interests include effective teaching practices, teacher training, and program evaluation.

Rachel Kohnke is a doctoral student in Educational Research at the University of Pittsburgh and a Research Assistant on the Teacher Center Project. She earned her Master's degree in Special Education at the University of Illinois. Her professional career includes teaching learning disabled students in public and private school settings and being an educational diagnostic consultant to teachers and parents. Over the past few years she has participated in various research projects in the public schools, including a review of procedures for implementing P.L. 94–142, The Education for All Handicapped Children Act of 1975, evaluation of a school improvement program, evaluation of a mixed-category special education instructional program, and evaluation of an inservice teacher training program.

1 Designing a Program for the Learning Disabled Adolescent

The past decade has seen a tremendous growth in programming for adolescents with learning disabilities (LD) as school districts have undertaken to comply with the mandate of Public Law 94–142, The Education for All Handicapped Children Act of 1975. Some of the students in these new programs were in special education LD classes while in elementary school but they entered middle school and high school still lacking a mastery of basic literacy and/or numeracy skills. Other students were not identified as LD until they reached adolescence and were unable to cope with the complexity of the secondary school and its content-subject classes. Whatever the source of the population, LD programs at the secondary level have grown disproportionately to the growth of services for other handicapping conditions at other age levels (Smith-Davis, Burke, & Noel, 1984).

Like LD programs at the elementary level, these new secondary programs are populated with an ill-defined, diverse set of students who may be characterized as passive learners (Torgesen, 1982), lacking in motivation (Adelman, 1978), underachieving in academic skills, particularly in reading (Alley & Deshler, 1979), with poor social interaction skills (Sheldon, Sherman, Hazel, Meyen, & Schumaker, 1982), poor ability to understand the varied demands of the secondary school (Deshler, Alley, & Carlson, 1980), and poor organizational skills (Silverman, Zigmond, & Sansone, 1981). These LD students are indeed a heterogeneous group in need of a wide and diverse set of curricular interventions.

PROGRAM OPTIONS AT THE SECONDARY SCHOOL LEVEL

In response to the demand for public school services for LD adolescents, a number of programming approaches, or models, have been proposed. These models tend to differ along two broad dimensions: (1) the amount of time for which LD students are assigned to receive instruction from the special education teacher, and (2) the extent to which the curriculum for these students is "special," that is, different from the curriculum offered to nonspecial education students in high school. Figure 1 represents these two dimensions for a high school that schedules seven class periods per day. The temporal dimension of assignment to special education instruction is represented vertically. LD students may be assigned to the special education teacher for no time at all (e.g., zero periods) or very little time (e.g., one period) or for an entire school day (e.g., seven periods). The extent to which the special education teacher uses a "special" curriculum is represented by the horizontal axis in Figure 1. Thus, the curriculum may be completely novel (7 on the horizontal axis), or it may be only a slight adaptation of the curriculum used in the mainstream (0 to 1 on the horizontal axis).

The temporal and curricular dimensions of programs provide a useful framework from which to analyze program options. We will

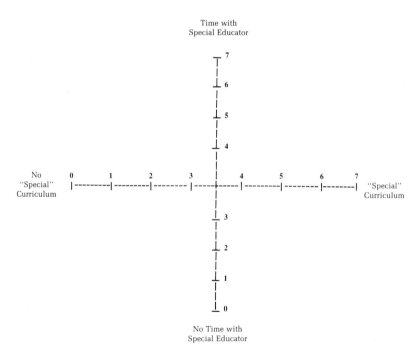

FIGURE 1. Framework for Categorizing Program Options at the Secondary Level.

briefly review service delivery models for secondary LD students currently in use across the country and catalog them within this framework. Then we will discuss the factors that influence the selection of program emphasis for LD adolescents.

The Resource Room Model—Novel Curriculum

The most popular administrative arrangement for LD students in high school programs is in the resource room model (Deshler, Lowrey, & Alley, 1979) in which students spend one or two class periods per day with a special education teacher and five or six class periods per day in the mainstream. Often, the curriculum presented to students by the resource room teacher is not typical of what is taught in high school, although the LD teacher may make use of high school textbooks and information on actual mainstream setting demands. The resource room curriculum may include basic skills remediation, survival skills lessons, instruction on learning strategies, or some combination of these three. This model would be placed on the lower right-hand quadrant of the graphic representation of program options: it involves up to two periods per day with the special educator (Vertical 2) and a very novel curriculum (Horizontal 6) (Figure 2).

In resource room programs which emphasize remediation of basic skills, the argument is made that LD adolescents will not benefit

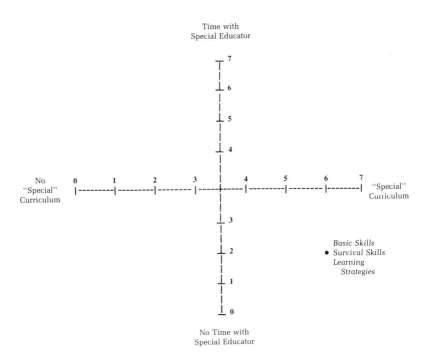

FIGURE 2. Program Options at the Secondary Level.

from high school books and assignments if they have not mastered certain basic word attack, reading comprehension, writing, or math computation skills. Competence in basic literacy and numeracy is viewed as a necessity for independent functioning during and after high school, and the resource room is viewed as the last opportunity for achieving this competence. Instruction in reading, written expression, and/or math may be similar to that found in elementary LD programs. Emphasis is placed on the use of direct instructional procedures and mastery learning (Goodman & Mann, 1976), on designing instruction that is explicit and highly intense (Meyen & Lehr, 1980), and on utilizing reinforcement strategies to increase motivation (Cox, 1980).

In resource room programs which emphasize survival skills (see Silverman et al., 1981), at least some portion of the time students spend with the special education teacher is devoted to explicit instruction in appropriate school behavior, teacher-pleasing behaviors, and study skills. Students are taught to analyze the setting demands of the high school and their typical behavioral responses to these demands. Then students are helped to learn alternative response patterns that increase their ability to cope in the mainstream. Survival skills instruction may utilize group counseling techniques or group goal-setting and feedback strategies as well as didactic approaches.

In resource room programs which emphasize instruction in learning strategies, students learn *how to learn*. Students are shown how to "make use of their existing academic skills in a strategically optimal fashion so that content information can be acquired, manipulated, stored, retrieved, and expressed" (Deshler, Schumaker, Lenz, & Ellis, 1984, p. 173). Task-specific strategies, techniques, rules, or principles are developed by the resource room teacher or adapted from those found in the growing literature on learning strategies and taught to the student following a prescribed series of steps (Deshler, Alley, Warner, & Schumaker, 1981). Students are encouraged to use the strategies while in the resource room and to extend their use to task demands of mainstream academic settings.

The Resource Room Model—Tutoring

Sometimes the role of the resource room teacher is defined to allow for the provision of "back up" instruction to LD students in mainstream content subjects. Areas of instruction are usually those subjects in which the LD student is having difficulty or failing. The LD resource room teacher's major responsibility is to help the student achieve a passing grade in his or her mainstream classes (Deshler et al., 1979). Instructional goals are defined by the course of study each student pursues in regular education. There are no special curriculum materials associated with this approach since the textbooks,

4

worksheets, and assignments of the mainstream teacher are the focuses of instruction. This program model belongs in the lower left-hand quadrant of the program options graph: No novel curricula are taught to the student by the special education teacher (Horizontal 0) but the student spends one or two class periods per day being tutored by the special education teacher (Vertical 1) (Figure 3).

Sometimes the tutorial approach is combined with cooperative planning (Riegel, 1980) in which the resource room teacher works with the mainstream teacher to develop alternative, compensatory mechanisms for the LD student to use in managing his or her regular classes. For example, the student may be permitted to tape lectures rather than take notes (Mosby, 1980), or to have chapter tests and final exams administered by the resource teacher in the resource room to permit more time, or to have oral presentation of the test questions and the answers (Figure 3).

Self-Contained Class—Novel Curriculum

The third most popular approach to secondary school programming (after basic skills instruction and tutoring) identified by Deshler and his colleagues in a survey published in 1979 is the Functional Curriculum approach. Here the major emphasis is on equipping LD students to function in society after graduation from high school.

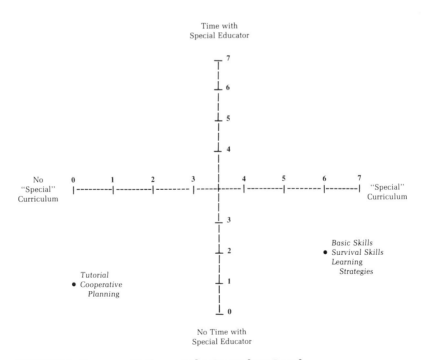

FIGURE 3. Program Options at the Secondary Level.

The regular curriculum of the high school is deemed inappropriate for LD students, so they are assigned to special education teachers for virtually the entire school day and are taught a different curriculum more suited to the students' needs. The new curriculum may focus on instruction in consumer information, filling out job application forms, mobility skills, community awareness, and prevocational and vocational preparation. This program option would fall in the extreme upper right-hand quadrant of the program options graph (Figure 4).

Self-Contained Class—Standard High School Curriculum

Hartwell, Wiseman, and Van Reusen (1979) have designed a programming option that maintains the same content objectives as the regular high school curriculum but varies the mode of presentation and the format of instruction to adapt to the special needs of LD students. The approach involves changing the conditions and settings of learning rather than changing the curriculum or the competencies of the learner. The Parallel Alternate Curriculum makes heavy use of film and other nonprint materials for presentation of content and alternatives to pencil-and-paper tests for evaluation of student progress.

Because the content coverage matches the mainstream curriculum and students spend almost full time with the special education teacher

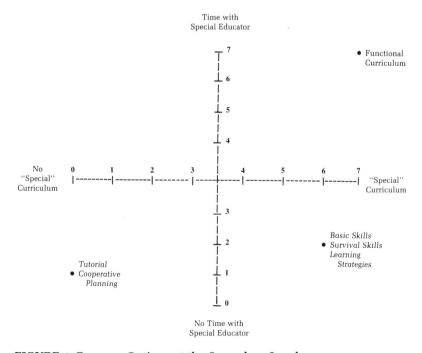

FIGURE 4. Program Options at the Secondary Level.

6

(as many as five periods per day), the Parallel Alternate Curriculum would be placed on the upper left hand quadrant of the graph (Vertical 5, Horizontal 0) (Figure 5).

Consultation Model

In a consultation model of secondary level special education services, the special education teacher works as a consultant to the regular education teachers or as a member of the mainstream instructional team (Miller & Sabatino, 1978; Lilly & Givens-Ogle, 1981; Idol-Maestas, 1983; Evans, 1980; McGlothlin, 1981; Knight, Meyers, Paolucci-Whitcomb, Hasazi, & Nevin, 1981). In the purest applications of the consultation model, no direct segregated special education services are provided for LD students. Efforts are made to "change the system" (Weiderholt & McEntire, 1980, pp. 2–3), rather than change the child. Consultants try to get mainstream teachers to adjust their instruction and instructional demands to accommodate the LD students successfully within their mainstream classes. This model belongs on the extreme lower left-hand quadrant of the graph representing the standard curriculum for LD students (Horizontal 7) with no time spent with a special education teacher (Vertical 0) (Figure 6).

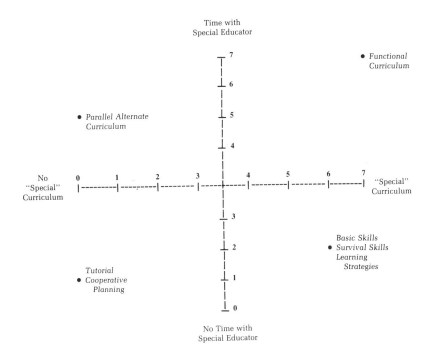

FIGURE 5. Program Options at the Secondary Level.

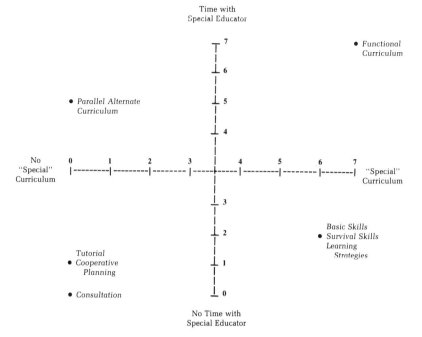

FIGURE 6. Program Options at the Secondary Level.

Work Study Model

The work study model emphasizes instruction in job and career-related skills and supervised on-the-job experiences as part of the school day. Students typically spend half of each day on a job and the remainder of the day studying material related to job success. The vocational curriculum may be provided by mainstream vocational educators or by LD teachers trained in vocational education for the handicapped. An LD teacher might also serve as a work coordinator, obtaining and supervising job placements for the LD students. If the job training program is taught by regular educators, this program would be placed just below the horizontal axis and to the left of the vertical (Vertical 3.5; Horizontal 3.5) to indicate that half of each school day is spent in regular education and on a regular education curriculum. If job training is the responsibility of special educators, the programs would be placed above the horizontal axis and to the right of the vertical indicating an alternative vocational education curriculum taught for half of each school day by special educators (Figure 7).

A review of Figure 7 illustrates the differences among the program models for secondary level LD students. In two programs, students spend a lot of time with the special education teacher (Functional Curriculum and Parallel Alternate Curriculum). Time in special ed-

8

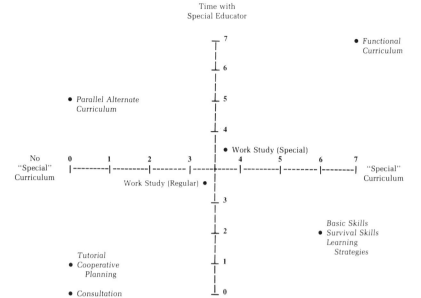

FIGURE 7. Program Options at the Secondary Level.

ucation is more limited in the remaining options. In some of the options, the curriculum is very different from that taught in the mainstream (learning strategies, basic skills, school survival skills, functional curriculum); in others, the special education curriculum derives from the mainstream curriculum. How does one choose among these models?

SELECTING AN APPROPRIATE LD PROGRAM

The choice of how much time students will spend in an LD program, or what to teach students once they are there may not be under the control of the LD teacher. Many factors influence the decision about program emphasis (Alley & Deshler, 1979; Brandis & Halliwell, 1980; Goodman & Mann, 1976; Wiseman, 1981). These factors can be grouped into three categories: (1) administrative practices, (2) teacher orientation, and (3) student characteristics.

Administrative Practices

Although ideally each high school should have available program options ranging from enrollment in a self-contained class for the whole school day to mainstream class enrollment for the whole day, in reality program choices in any one school tend to be quite limited

(Cruickshank, 1977; Ryor, 1978). The decision to operate the LD program as a resource room or as a series of self-contained, content-subject classes or as a consultation program is generally made at the administrative level. This decision then influences class size assignments, scheduling of students, and expectations of the school administrative and teaching staffs. Furthermore, if the school administrators select a direct service model and leave no time in the special education teacher's daily schedule for consultation with the mainstream teacher, it is unlikely that the LD teacher will find cooperative planning or consultation viable program options. However, within the temporal constraints imposed by administrative practices, the LD teacher *can* make curricular choices around the extent of "special" education to be provided.

Teacher Orientation

The factors that will most influence teachers' choices of curricula are their own training and experiences. Many secondary level LD teachers were prepared in teacher education programs which emphasized instruction at the elementary level. Strong commitments to basic skill teaching may be related to lack of exposure to alternatives. Teachers who have had no training in consultation may not opt to include working with mainstream teachers as a component of the LD program. Teachers who were prepared as content specialists at the secondary level may feel most comfortable in the Parallel Alternate Curriculum model or in a resource room tutoring program. However, decisions about curriculum and program emphasis should not be based upon a teacher's comfort level. Rather, program choices should be based on identified student needs.

Student Characteristics

The most important factors to be considered in the selection of program options for the LD student are the student's history of special education and growth patterns in academic skills before high school, the student's and the parents' goals for post-high school, and the student's behavioral responses to high school demands. Initially, a review of a student's records will reveal the extent of previous basic skill instruction in special education and the patterns of growth in previous years. If a student has recently been assigned to the LD program, or has been in an elementary or middle school program but has made steady progress in improving basic skills, the teacher would do well to continue with basic skills focus. If, however, the student has not made progress in academic skills, that is, has reached a plateau in the development of basic skills competence, other curriculum options may be more appropriate.

Likewise, if a student enters the high school program with literacy skills at the fifth to sixth grade level, learning strategies could be included in the curriculum plan (Deshler et al., 1979). If, however, the student's reading levels are considerably below this level, learning strategies will probably not be effective.

Learning strategies combined with tutoring might be selected if an LD student is college bound and has basic competencies (to sixth grade) in reading and math. A parallel alternate curriculum model may be selected for students who are capable of mastering the content of high school courses but unable to manage either the format of, or the competition in, a mainstream curriculum. Work study or functional curricula may be more appropriate for students who are not college bound and who will want to leave high school with job-related skills.

In selecting program options, the teacher should also consider the student's ability to adapt to the demands of the high school setting. For students who are getting into trouble with school authorities or are not completing school assignments appropriately, training in "survival skills" such as behavior control, teacher-pleasing behaviors, and study skills (Silverman et al., 1981) may be appropriate.

Ideally, any high school program for LD students would be comprehensive and draw upon several models, implementing each component to a greater or lesser degree depending on the administrative practices of the school, the teacher's orientation, and the particular needs of individual students. This kind of approach was taken by Zigmond (1978) in the model program developed for secondary school-age students in the Pittsburgh Public Schools and replicated subsequently in various school districts across the United States. Because Zigmond and her coworkers were strongly committed to the concept of mainstreaming, they utilized program components from the bottom half of Figure 7. They recommended a resource room setting for instruction in basic skills, school survival skills, and learning strategies, with time in the resource room limited to not more than two class periods each day. They also recommended consultation/cooperative planning with regular educators as an integral part of each LD student's program, and vocational education for LD students when they reached the eleventh grade. The IMPRESS Training Manual (1984), developed in Florida and supported by the Florida Department of Education, is a second example of an eclectic, comprehensive, secondary-level LD model. It incorporates curriculum components from all quadrants of Figure 7: learning strategies, parallel skills, oral and silent reading fluency and remediation of basic skills, as well as a parent participation component.

Such comprehensive models of service delivery are more costly, require more training of staff, and more flexibility in the scheduling of LD students. However, by making a variety of options available, a school district can provide a truly appropriate and individualized educational opportunity for each LD high school student.

2 Planning for Instruction

The decision about which curriculum components to include in an LD student's high school special education program is generally made on the basis of data gathered during the referral, classification and placement procedures, and a review of student records. The decision is reflected in the student's Individualized Education Program (IEP). But once broad domains of instruction have been selected, the teacher must develop detailed instructional plans for each student. Three aspects of instructional planning will be considered here: how to assess individual student instructional needs, how to motivate students to attend to instruction, and how to organize classrooms and manage student behavior to maximize classroom control.

ASSESSMENT OF INDIVIDUAL STUDENT INSTRUCTIONAL NEEDS

Assessment of individual student needs is central to the concept of an individualized educational program. In such an assessment, data are collected on what skills the student has and has not mastered and how the student approaches the learning tasks. The results of the assessment help the teacher decide where to begin instruction within a curriculum domain and how to design learning tasks for the student.

There is evidence to suggest that special education teachers, because of their training and orientation, learn a great deal about their students just from daily, casual observations of student behavior. However, these teacher judgments are not perfect. In fact, recent studies have shown that most special education teachers cannot determine levels of student performance or skill needs accurately enough for planning instruction on the basis of casual, unsystematic observations alone (Utley, 1982; Fuchs & Fuchs, 1984). Teachers need to record data on student errors or correct responses; writing things down in some systematic way seems to be an essential element in making more accurate evaluations. For this reason, many researchers and practitioners are recommending that a formalized assessment procedure be utilized by teachers as the basis of their planning effort.

There are two ways in which teachers can obtain assessment data that might be useful in instructional planning: the teacher may use formal assessment procedures or informal ones. Formal assessments utilize published tests which have very specific instructions for administration and scoring. These tests generally yield age equivalent scores or grade equivalent scores that are based on the performance of some sample of students on whom the test was normed. Informal assessment procedures utilize teacher-made tests, observation protocols, trial teachings, skill checklists, rating scales, or interviews. Informal tests are preferred over formal, standardized tests because the informal tests are curriculum specific, that is, they allow the teacher to evaluate samples of student behavior in relation to specific instructional concerns. Formal tests, on the other hand, test knowledge or skills across a whole domain but are not specifically related to a single curriculum. Informal assessments focus on student achievement in relation to the demands of the environment rather than in relation to a norm group. They also allow for maximal adaptation of administrative procedures, content, materials, and scoring criteria to meet the needs of particular assessment situations (Bennett, 1982). Formal tests, administered properly, do not allow the same flexibility.

To carry out an informal assessment, teachers may opt to use direct systematic data collection techniques. Systematic classroom observation of specific student behaviors is especially useful in understanding instructional needs regarding social skills, work habits, appropriate classroom behaviors, self-help skills, and job performance. Direct systematic observations have the advantage of assessing behaviors in the settings in which they occur, rather than in an artificial environment. But the teacher needs to be careful to specify the behaviors to be observed and to develop observation protocols and record forms on which to record and summarize findings if the information collected is to be useful in planning instruction (Keller, 1983).

Another way to collect informal assessment data is to provide the student with a task to complete and to analyze both student behaviors while doing the task and student error patterns on the final product. Zigmond, Vallecorsa, and Silverman (1983) propose a 12-step strategy for this type of assessment for instructional planning and recommend its use particularly when academic skill performance data are sought. Their procedure appears to be "formal," because it is systematic and orderly. But it is an informal assessment procedure utilizing teacher-made and curriculum-embedded tests and placing heavy emphasis on evaluating student performance rather than on final test scores. It also calls for considerable preliminary decision making and planning before any tasks/tests are administered. In the first five steps of the 12-step strategy, the teacher decides what curriculum area is to be assessed, develops a skill hierarchy to represent that curricular area, decides where along the hierarchy to begin the assessment, and selects or develops an appropriate criterion-referenced assessment. Administering the assessment is step six in the strategy. Steps seven, eight, and nine involve the teacher in evaluating student performance and analyzing error patterns. The outcome is a guess about skill deficits that is tested out in step 10 using informal probes. In steps 11 and 12 the teacher converts assessment information into instructional plans.

The approach of Zigmond and her colleagues relies on systematic error analysis of student responses on the tasks that the student is given during the surveys (step six) and the probes (step 10). Teachers can also employ systematic error analysis of classroom work samples to obtain meaningful data on whether their instructional program is working. At best, program planning decisions based on initial assessments are hypotheses; frequent, direct measurements of student classroom performance tell the teacher if the instructional decisions that were made on the basis of the preliminary informal assessments were correct. Mirkin, Fuchs, and Deno (1982) have developed a very useful model within which teachers can design their own direct and frequent measurement system. The model guides the teacher's decisions on what to measure, how to measure, and how to use the data to make instructional programs more effective. Their data show that the use of direct and frequent recording of student performance by the teacher can lead to significant improvements in skill acquisition.

In 1976, Morrissey and Semmel noted that "the teacher's ability to make decisions, probably more than any other variable, affects how and what the child will learn" (p. 14). Assessment of student instructional needs and student responsiveness to instruction can contribute significantly to the quality of the teacher's decision making. Assessment of individual instructional needs should have a central place in the LD program. It can have a profound impact on the educational achievement of LD students at the secondary school level.

MOTIVATING STUDENTS TO ATTEND TO INSTRUCTION

A critical area to consider when planning to teach LD adolescents is motivation. The best made decisions about what to teach and the most skillful applications of how to teach will only be successful if the targeted students are motivated to learn. While this concept applies to students in general, it is especially important for secondary LD students for whom learning, and school in general, have been frustrating and unrewarding experiences. Traditional school motivators like teacher praise and grades may not be effective with these students (Marsh, Gearheart, & Gearheart, 1978). Instead, high school LD students need to be motivated to engage in learning tasks through careful selection of teaching materials and tasks or by giving students reasons for trying once again to learn something academic (Marsh et al., 1978).

We recommend that secondary LD teachers design lessons that draw on students' interests, are mature in content, pragmatic, and have success built into them. LD adolescents are at a stage in their development where they are increasingly interested in who they are and in what is happening to them. They tend to enjoy materials or subject matter that deal with being an adolescent. Teachers can capitalize on this interest.

The idea of using students' interests in selecting materials or subject matter is not new. Teachers have often reported success with adolescents when teaching them to read using a driver's training manual, a car mechanics magazine, or stories about sports, fashion, dating, or family problems. But this approach can also be applied to other instructional areas. Written language activities in which students write about their feelings and opinions in letters, journals, or autobiographies may prove more motivating to students than the more traditional writing exercises. Math skills can be taught through students' interests in sports (computing batting averages) or fashion (developing clothes allowances). Spelling lessons which permit students to select words they want to know how to spell are often more successful than those which utilize a basic spelling list. Trying to motivate students by using their interests may not be possible in every teaching situation, but it is often an effective way to get students involved in learning.

In addition to being motivated by materials that deal with adolescence, LD high school students appreciate subject matter that seems mature, especially when, by contrast, the skill levels at which they are working may be rather elementary. Reading the newspaper, reading about careers, writing checks, figuring out tax forms, and completing job applications are among the many adult-like tasks that can be vehicles for basic skills instruction. The maturity level of the topic may also contribute to a more positive student self-image.

To help with the selection of teaching materials and tasks, LD teachers should take the time to find out what students find interesting. Teachers can use formal interest inventories or simply engage the students in social conversations. Both procedures not only provide the teacher with invaluable information but also show the students that the teacher considers their interests important and worthwhile.

In addition to motivating secondary LD students by using their interests, LD teachers should make it clear that the skills being worked on are useful. Learning seems more "legitimate" to students at the secondary level if they can be convinced that:

1. They need the skills to get a job.
2. They need the skills to perform on a job.
3. They need the skills to survive as an adult.
4. They need this particular skill before other, more desirable skills can be learned.
5. They need the skills to be mainstreamed into a particular regular class.
6. They need the skills for college or some type of postsecondary training.
7. They need the skills to complete the courses and earn the credits required for high school graduation.
8. They need the skills to enjoy or participate in a desired leisure time activity.
9. They need the skills to function like their normal peers.
10. They need the skills to participate in extracurricular school activities.

Students can be made aware of these reasons for learning through group or individual discussions. Frequent reminders of why learning is important may be needed. Whenever possible, students should be given opportunities to see how the acquisition of skills or knowledge has benefited other students in the LD program or students who have already graduated from the program. A few encouraging comments from a respected peer are often more worthwhile than a lecture from the teacher; they help students realize that others with similar disabilities have been able to learn and succeed.

Since previous attempts at learning have often been unreinforcing experiences for LD students, teachers need to find ways to reward students immediately for initial efforts to perform academically. Students then may begin to find the learning process less onerous and may become encouraged to continue trying. While traditional reinforcers may not be effective with this population, more unusual reinforcers are (Belcastro, 1977; Dolly & Pittman, 1976; Egner, 1974; Marsh et al., 1978). These reinforcers include:

1. Tokens for achievement.
2. Self-recording or charting of academic progress.
3. Grades in school tied to allowances at home.
4. Time to spend in a game center or recreational activity.
5. Time to play tapes or records.

6. Opportunity to schedule when academic lessons take place.
7. Use of a "bank account" to buy privileges or free time.
8. Tangible reinforcers such as fast food coupons, magazines, and movie tickets.
9. Exemption from an additional assignment or homework.
10. Extra time for lunch or for a break.

Teachers usually use these reinforcers on an individual basis, but teachers may also want to consider using some form of group contingency to capitalize on the influence of peers and peer pressure among adolescents. For example, several teachers we know have successfully used a timer which is set to go off at random intervals, and have then rewarded the whole group if all or most of the students are on task when the timer rings. Other teachers have set individual academic goals for students, yet have provided reinforcement only if everyone in the group reaches his or her individual goal.

With either individual or group reinforcements, teachers need to view the provision of reinforcers along a continuum. At first, students may need to be reinforced frequently for their efforts to learn. Gradually, it may be possible to withdraw extrinsic reinforcers because as students experience success they will become more internally motivated to learn.

ORGANIZING THE CLASSROOM AND MANAGING STUDENT BEHAVIOR TO MAXIMIZE CLASSROOM CONTROL

Before there can be successful instruction in an LD classroom at the secondary level (or, for that matter, in any classroom at any level), the teacher must have things under control. Students cannot learn and teachers cannot teach amidst chaos. Control is especially important in a special education classroom because, unlike most secondary classrooms, the secondary special education room is a place where more than one type of instructional activity is likely to be going on at any given time. Because of the variety of instructional activities that will need to be planned, the LD teacher will have to develop an organization and management system. Each teacher's system will be different because it will reflect that teacher's unique instructional style as well as the particular needs of his or her students.

In this section we will discuss organizational issues such as structuring the classroom environment, scheduling student and teacher time, establishing classroom routines, and collecting and maintaining classroom records. We will conclude this section with a discussion of behavior management strategies that can be used to avoid and avert discipline problems that interfere with the instructional process. We will begin by reviewing some general practices that undergird any teacher's approach to classroom organization.

Guidelines for Classroom Organization and Management

1. Keep classroom procedures as simple and easy as possible. A teacher's time and energy should not be used up in "directing traffic" or completing paperwork. Teacher time is best spent in delivering instruction. If recordkeeping systems or reward systems are overly complicated or difficult to complete, both the teacher and the students will be reluctant to use them. If the number of rules that students must follow are limited to those that are essential to personal safety and courtesy, students will be more likely to remember them, to feel that the teacher is being reasonable, and to follow them.

2. Develop recordkeeping systems that serve more than one purpose. Secondary special education teachers do not only have their own needs to consider. They must also adhere to their school's policies and to state reporting regulations. Therefore, it is advantageous to coordinate these various responsibilities. Designing student assignment sheets that can also fulfill the school's requirement for lesson plans helps. Using a grading system that incorporates recordkeeping on progress in academic work and behavior management can reduce the number of forms a secondary LD teacher may have to complete.

3. Involve the students in the management of the classroom whenever possible (Long & Frye, 1977). Students at the secondary level need to learn to use and control their own environment. By having students take attendance, or correct their own or their peers' assignments, teachers can save themselves considerable time and provide their students with valuable experiences.

4. Be consistent in adhering to classroom procedures. Once routines have been established for securing assignments and for turning in completed work make sure that students know that they will be expected to follow the procedure at all times. Then, be consistent in demanding and reinforcing compliance. This consistency helps to reduce any confusion or uncertainty that students may have. When students know what to expect they feel more secure within the classroom setting. In fact, it is a good idea to introduce and institute the classroom routines at the very beginning of the year and, to the extent possible, maintain them throughout the school year.

5. Establish priorities for the use of planning time. Lesson planning, recordkeeping, and other paperwork need to be scheduled so that they can be completed within a reasonable time frame. However, it will not be possible to do everything at the same time. Determine what are the more critical responsibilities and what can be put off to a later date. Setting priorities and scheduling time during which a few tasks are accomplished each day can save the teacher from feeling overwhelmed.

6. Base classroom management strategies on the needs, behaviors, and characteristics of the students in the LD classroom (Sabatino, Sabatino, & Mann, 1983). The procedures used by the previous teacher or observed in use by other teachers may not be applicable to the group of students who now comprise a particular instructional group. Management strategies must take into account the students' interests, their attention span, and their ability to get along with one another. LD secondary teachers need to find management strategies that not only work well but that are comfortable for them and for their students.

7. Adhere to the policies and procedures of the school. The daily schedule for special education students should not conflict with that of the rest of the school. School regulations regarding absences and tardiness should not be compromised by the LD teacher. Not only does this help the LD teacher in his or her relationships with the rest of the high school faculty and with the administrative staff, but it also helps the students know that the LD program is an integral part of the school.

Organizing the Environment, the Students, and the Teacher

With these principles in mind, the teacher must set about organizing the room, the students, and himself or herself to maximize control. Tasks include structuring the physical space of the classroom, scheduling student and teacher time, and establishing classroom routines. These planning activities support the instructional program and make the classroom "work."

Structuring the Classrooom Environment

LD adolescents and their teachers can be influenced by the classroom environment. The physical plan of the classroom can help or hinder the LD teacher in maintaining a good working atmosphere. Therefore, the LD teacher needs to consider what would be the most practical, as well as attractive, arrangement of the room. Most teachers find it useful to:

1. Request a room within the mainstream of the school.
2. Arrange desks, work tables, file cabinets, study carrels, and bookshelves so that there are areas for teacher directed activities, independent work, and "special projects," and so that students can move about the room from one activity to another with minimal disruption of other students' work.
3. Place instruction materials and supplies where they can be retrieved easily by the students.
4. Designate wall space throughout the room on which to display student work, appropriate posters, pictures, slogans, school news, and announcements.

5. Arrange student seating to take into consideration the number of students in the room at one time, the way they interact, and the type of instruction that will be provided to them.
6. Place the teacher's desk so as to facilitate constant visual supervision of the room and students.
7. Avoid creating areas out of the teacher's view where students can get into trouble.

Deciding on an effective classroom arrangement may take time initially, but it is worth the effort. A disorganized classroom can hinder good instruction and prevent learning. The LD room should be neat, attractive, and organized so that the environment is conducive to hard work and learning.

Scheduling Teacher and Student Time

Two basic types of instructional activities go on in an LD classroom: teacher directed instruction and independent seatwork. These activities serve different purposes. The introduction of new material is best accomplished with teacher direction, while drill and practice of skills can take place during independent seatwork. In planning for instruction, teachers must consider the particular learning needs of each student and choose the type of activity which best facilitates continued progress toward instructional goals. The balance between teacher directed and independent activities prescribed for a given student will depend on the individual needs of that student although, for reasons we will give in a subsequent section of this monograph, for most students the schedule should favor teacher directed activities.

Scheduling of teacher and student time is one of the most important planning tasks of the LD teacher. The schedule should be practical and sensible but also flexible. First, the teacher should decide with whom he or she will spend time in direct instruction and for how long. Then the teacher should assign appropriate independent practice activities to the remaining students in the class. Flexibility in the schedule would allow for a shorter or longer teacher directed lesson depending on the responses of that instructional group and on the capabilities of the students who are working alone. Classroom routines should already be established so that the LD students can settle down to work without wondering what will happen next. Routines are an important part of the smooth functioning of any classroom (Leinhardt, Hammond, Weidman, & Figura, 1984).

Establishing Management Procedures

To make the schedule run smoothly, teachers should develop procedures that let the students know what they are to do, when to change activities, what to do if they need help, and what to do when their work has been completed. Here are some suggestions for developing these procedures.

1. *Letting students know what to do.* As students enter the LD secondary classroom they need to find out what their assignments are and whether they are to be working independently or with the teacher. Teachers could wait until all students are in the room and have settled down, then announce to the class how instruction that period will be organized for each student. Or, each student could pick up a work folder as he or she enters the class; a schedule or checklist in the folder would outline the tasks for the period. Or, students could report to a particular work station each day; a task card at the work station would indicate the list of tasks to be completed that period. Or, the teacher could establish a standard routine that, after a few weeks, needs no explanation.

2. *Telling students when to change activities.* Some teachers use a timer to indicate when students are to move on to the next activity. Other teachers find that scheduling activities into 15- or 20-minute time blocks is appropriate. Still others require students to complete an assignment before moving on, regardless of how much of the period it takes; students change activities when they are ready to do the next task.

3. *What students are to do if they need help with their seatwork.* Students need to know how they go about asking the teacher (or peers) for assistance without interrupting the teacher directed activities going on elsewhere in the room. To get help, a student could write his or her name on the board, take a number, or raise his or her hand. Whatever the system, timely breaks are needed in the teacher directed instruction to allow the teacher to attend to students who need help, and students need to have specific instructions about what they are to do while they are waiting for assistance.

4. *What students are to do when they finish a task.* Students need to know if they are to correct their own work (and if so, where the answer keys are kept), if they are to go on to another assignment, of if they may spend time in a "free time" activity while waiting for the rest of the class to get to the "change activity" point.

By establishing these classroom procedures, the LD teacher can provide an organizational framework that is efficient, conducive to learning, and that will also promote appropriate classroom behavior.

Developing and Maintaining Classroom Records

Since LD teachers need to keep records on many aspects of a student's educational program, their recordkeeping system needs to be as efficient as possible. Teachers should keep the numbers and kinds of forms to a minimum. All pertinent information on a student should be kept in one place so that it is readily accessible.

Most LD teachers use a file system to keep records on each of their students. An alternative would be to use a separate notebook or folder that contains all information on a particular student. Using different colored paper helps to organize various types of student data. Regardless, there are three critical features to any recordkeeping system. First, the teachers must be able to record accurately and efficiently all pertinent student information. Second, the teacher should not have to write the same information more than once. Third, the teacher should be able to retrieve recorded information quickly for use in planning or for sharing with parents, the student, or other educators.

Managing Student Behavior

A sound behavior-management system is a critical component of a special education classroom for LD adolescents. While the focus of an LD classroom is generally on instruction, behavior problems may have to be considered and dealt with before instruction can be effective (Mann, Goodman, & Wiederholt, 1978). This requires that the LD teacher learn how to prevent behavior problems, understand why they occur, and know what to do to solve them.

To prevent behavior problems, teachers should establish the rules and regulations that govern students while they are in the classroom. The decision about what these should be needs to be made before the beginning of school so that the rules can be presented to students as soon as they begin their program. Rules should be written and posted, then discussed with each student individually. This will serve to clarify any questions or misconceptions about the kind of behavior that the teacher expects. Rules should include common school-appropriate behaviors such as being on time, using proper language, and not talking out in class. In addition, teachers may want to add specific rules that reflect some of their personal preferences or management concerns. The important thing is that there are rules that are reviewed often, and that the consequences for breaking the rules are specified. In this way, students will know what the limits are and what will happen if these limits are violated.

A second way to prevent behavior problems is for LD teachers to get to know and understand their students. Spending time reviewing a student's permanent folder, psychological report, and anecdotal records can provide useful information regarding the student's behavior and his or her responses to various school related situations. Teachers can begin to recognize or anticipate academic and/or social situations that are frustrating or stressful to a particular student. Avoiding these situations whenever possible or structuring the environment to lessen their impact can do much to help prevent outbursts of undesirable behavior.

Teachers can also observe the students as they struggle with new learning and watch and listen to them in social encounters to determine the kind of structure and pacing they may need in order to act appropriately in class. Behavioral characteristics of students such as their attention span, frustration level, and reinforcement needs will become apparent after a period of observation. With prior knowledge of these characteristics the teacher can design more appropriate instruction.

A third way of preventing behavior problems involves establishing a "work-like" atmosphere. By this we mean that students know that the special education room is a place where serious work is to be accomplished. It is not simply a "break" from the regular education class schedule. Students also need to know that "work-like" behavior is expected in the LD room, and that certain routines and procedures must be followed. Providing students with enough work to keep them busy and making them accountable for its completion indicates to students that they are responsible for meeting deadlines and that their work will be reviewed and evaluated regularly. Students also need to realize the importance of practicing good work habits so that getting started on work and seeing it through to its completion become automatic responses. Not only will these behaviors prevent behavior problems, but they will also prepare the students for mainstream classes and for future employment.

Although teachers can do a great deal to prevent behavior problems, some will still occur. Before trying to solve these problems, it is important that teachers understand the reasons behind the inappropriate behaviors. Zigmond, Brownlee, Laurie, and Stanek (1981) identified several reasons for inappropriate student behaviors:

1. Students are imitating or modeling behavior they have observed somewhere else. They have learned bad habits in the same way that they have learned good ones.
2. Students are receiving some kind of "payoff" or reward for the display of undesirable behavior. If they were not being rewarded, such behavior would not continue.
3. Students are receiving attention from the teacher or from their peers. This attention, even if it is negative, may be reinforcing to students who have not learned how to get attention in more positive ways.
4. Students are avoiding doing what they have been assigned to do. The behavioral disruptions are a more desirable activity than listening to instruction or working on assignments.
5. Students are not aware of the classroom rules or of the teacher's expectations. They may not be picking up subtle clues from the teacher that they are misbehaving.

6. Students are not concerned with the rewards or the punishment that have been specified by the teacher regarding misbehavior. They may not view the consequences as important or as valuable enough to warrant positive behavior or self-control.

This list is certainly not complete. It outlines only the most common causes of misbehavior. Teachers are encouraged to use this list only as a point of reference and to add to it as individual and unique reasons for misbehavior arise. The point is that there is always a reason why a student is misbehaving and that understanding the reason is the first step toward solving the problem.

Once the reason for the misbehavior is understood, teachers must set about correcting the behavior problem. To do that, Zigmond et al. (1981) suggest that teachers answer several critical questions:

What is the student doing that is inappropriate?
When is the student displaying the inappropriate behavior?
How often does the inappropriate behavior occur?
What are the payoffs or rewards the student is receiving for maintaining this behavior?

To get the answers to these questions the teacher may have to take direct observational data on the student's behavior for several days. (See Kerr & Nelson [1983] for very good examples of how to do that.) Once the teacher has the data, he or she will also have a clear picture of the behavior problem and some clues for figuring out how to proceed.

Several options for correcting less severe types of behavior problems can be readily implemented (Zigmond et al., 1981):

1. Restate the rules and the consequences to the misbehaving students. Students who may not have intentionally violated an established classroom rule may simply need this kind of reminder. By indicating what a more appropriate behavior would be, the teacher can help these students understand why their behavior was inappropriate.
2. Restructure the environment so that the misbehavior will be less likely to occur. Changing a student's seat or providing a visual clue when a student begins to misbehave can correct some behavior problems and can demonstrate to the student that the teacher is willing to help him or her overcome the difficulty.
3. Ignore inappropriate behavior if it seems the student is misbehaving in order to get attention. This strategy will work only if the student's peers also ignore the inappropriate behavior and if the student receives attention when appropriate behavior is displayed.

4. Punish the student for misbehaving. The negative consequence delivered must be meaningful to the student, must be delivered immediately, and must be explained to the student so it is clear why the punishment is being administered.

When the four strategies just mentioned do not work, teachers need to begin teaching the student a new behavior which can replace the inappropriate one. Doing so takes more time and planning but the results can be quite successful if certain steps are followed (Zigmond et al., 1981):

- Define the new behavior that the student is to perform. Be specific about what the student is to do and when the behavior is to be displayed. Break a long-term goal into smaller subgoals and focus initially on having the student work on one subgoal at a time.
- Identify the kinds of rewards that can be used to reinforce the performance of the new behavior. Specific rewards, whether things, privileges, or social activities, will need to be selected on an individual basis. The reward used must be of value to the student and must be realistic in terms of how much of the teacher's time or energy is needed to deliver it.
- Determine how to give the student the selected reward. Consider how often it needs to be delivered and exactly what the student needs to do in order to get the reward. Initially, accept and immediately reward imperfect attempts at the new behavior. As the student becomes more adept, the standards can be raised and more accurate displays of the new behavior can be expected. At some point, the frequency and immediacy of the rewards should be decreased so that the students begin to view the behavior itself as valuable. More intangible types of reinforcers, like praise or approval, can then be substituted for the more concrete rewards that may have been needed initially.

If these steps are followed and if the rewards are appropriately administered, teachers should begin to see the students making progress in controlling their behavior. If not, and we realize that this is possible, teachers may want to consider seeking help of an additional professional. This outsider could be another teacher, a counselor, an administrator, or the school psychologist. Often, an objective third party who has observed the student's behavior and who understands the situation can offer sound advice. His or her involvement alone, even if it just includes talking to the student about the behavior problem, may help to alleviate the situation.

In addition, at the secondary level, students should be involved in planning and managing their own behavior modification program (Mann et al., 1978). Any attempt which lets students know that they are responsible for their own behavior is worthwhile. We view both the seeking of outside support and the inclusion of the student in deciding what to do as constructive, positive, and caring approaches to dealing with adolescents whose behavior is interfering with their own learning or the learning of their peers.

Behavior management is one of the most important responsibilities of LD teachers. Steps should be taken to prevent behavior problems. But when problems do occur, a carefully planned and sensible approach will prove effective and will increase the chances a student has to learn.

3 Organizing Instruction to Maximize Student Learning

Much has been written about how to teach learning disabled students (Alley & Deshler, 1979; Lerner, 1976; Miller & Davis, 1982; Smith, 1983). In this section we will not restate these discussions. Rather, we will review what we have learned from research about significant variables that affect adolescent learning. Most of this research has been carried out in mainstream secondary settings with regular education students, and the findings have not found their way into very much of the LD literature. We believe, however, that this research is applicable to the LD setting and that teachers who incorporate these findings into their instructional plans are likely to develop better instructional programs for their students.

The primary job of any teacher is to structure and deliver instruction so as to maximize student learning. How instruction will proceed and whether the students will benefit from it depend on the decisions the teacher has made regarding elements in the teaching process that are known to affect student learning. These elements include time for student learning, teacher-student interactions, and lesson structure. This section provides a review of this research and its implications for the LD teacher.

MAXIMIZING THE TIME FOR STUDENT LEARNING

Research results have confirmed what good teachers have long known intuitively: what students learn from their classroom experiences depends on what they do during class time. This means that to maximize students' learning, students must be present for instruction, on task, and actively involved in learning. None of these is easy to achieve at the high school level.

Absence from school is a serious problem among high school students in general but particularly among learning disabled students (Zigmond, Levin, & Laurie, 1985; Zigmond, Kerr, Brown, & Harris, 1984). Stallings (1981) reported a number of strategies which can help reduce absentee rates at the secondary level (Stallings, 1981; Needels & Stallings, 1975). She suggests students are less likely to be absent if they perceive the classroom to be friendly and if they perceive the teacher to have high expectations for students. Absentee rates are reportedly also lower in classrooms where the teacher provides a lot of verbal instruction and where instruction is given to groups of students instead of one-on-one.

Getting students to come to school is the first step in providing them with opportunities to learn. The second step is to get them engaged in learning tasks. Since students have only a limited amount of time in any classroom, teachers have to organize time in a way that maximizes the amount of time students spend on their work and minimizes the amount of "down time."

Unfortunately, teachers cannot always manage to do this. We have found that a considerable portion of LD students' time is spent waiting for assignments or equipment, getting ready to work, straightening up after completing assignments, and being off task (Kohnke, Zigmond, & Miller, 1985; Zigmond et al., 1984). Others have found that classroom time can easily get taken up by transitions (Brophy & Evertson, 1974), the management of materials (Cooley & Leinhardt, 1980), or the management of student behavior (Brophy & Evertson, 1974). Research findings suggest that students make greater academic gains in activities (Brophy & Evertson, 1974). So, it is important that the LD teacher be vigilant about how class time is being spent and schedule as much working time as possible during each class period.

Of course, the amount of time *scheduled* for a specific learning activity is not what is important. It is the amount of time that students actually spend on the task that relates to achievement (Cooley & Leinhardt, 1980). We have already discussed the importance of having learning activities at the right level of difficulty for the students and the usefulness of informal assessments to determine skill needs. This will increase rates of on-task behavior. We have also described ways of motivating students to maintain their interest in and commitment to learning. There is also some research evidence to suggest that students learn more in classrooms where there are fewer disruptions (Coker, Lorentz, & Coker, 1976). Therefore, to encourage high levels of on-task behavior, teachers need to select tasks carefully (using appropriate informal assessments to determine level), motivate students to stay engaged, and manage disruptions efficiently so that student work is not interrupted.

There is general agreement that more learning will take place if students are not simply engaged, but actively involved, in instruction. Active participation may be defined as the consistent engagement of the minds of *all* the students, *all* the time with what is being learned (Pittsburgh Public Schools, 1985). The Hunter model (1974) proposes that learning tasks be planned which require as much overt participation by the student as possible. Discussion activities or questioning sessions are a direct means by which the teacher can encourage active student involvement. Covert activities such as listening, silent reading, or independent seatwork assignments need to be followed up with overt participation tasks, such as putting answers on the board or answering questions orally.

It is not only the students who need to be actively involved in the learning process. The teacher's direct involvement with students is also a significant variable in student learning. Students are known to achieve more in classes where they spend most of their time being *actively taught* or supervised by the teacher rather than working independently (Good & Brophy, in press). A study of remedial reading students at the secondary level (Stallings, 1981) compared classrooms of teachers whose students made high gains with classrooms of teachers whose students made low gains. The low-gains classrooms were typically those in which students worked independently on silent reading or written seatwork activities. Conversely, those classrooms which were organized into discussion, oral review activities, and oral reading activities showed highest student gains (Stallings & Kaskowitz, 1974; Sear, 1973). Frequent interactions with the teacher and active instruction from the teacher have been shown to be of particular importance for low-achieving students (Stallings, 1980a, 1980b, 1981).

These findings have several implications for the LD teacher. First, the teacher should plan more activities that provide direct instruction to students and fewer activities in which students are in charge of their own instruction or practicing independently. Second, the teacher should distribute direct instruction time to more students more of the time.

LD teachers have always been strongly committed to individualized, one-to-one instruction. This may not always be the most efficient distribution of the teacher's resources. A number of studies which have addressed the question of the efficacy of one-to-one instruction have found no evidence that it is superior to the other methods of remedial education (Cooley & Leinhardt, 1980; Leinhardt, 1977). Zigmond and her colleagues (Zigmond et al., 1984) have shown that when the LD secondary teacher organizes the resource room for one-to-one instruction, each student gets only about 5 minutes of instruction from the teacher each 45-minute class period (or perhaps 10 minutes of teacher directed instruction every other day), with the remaining time being spent in independent, self-directed practice tasks.

In the classroom where the teacher is occupied with one individual at a time, the other students are invariably left to work independently. To provide LD students with more teacher directed instruction, small group instruction will have to replace the one-to-one format. This does not necessarily mean that instruction should not be adapted to meet individual needs. However, the research findings suggest that such adaptation should be carried out in the context of teaching a small group. This is easiest if groups are developed which contain several students who are working on the same or similar skills. Through this kind of grouping, one teacher in a high school special education class increased student time in teacher directed instruction from an average of 9% of student learning time when instruction was delivered one-to-one, to 42% of student learning time with grouping (Zigmond, 1984). This teacher felt that she was still able to adjust to the individual needs of her students during group instruction by continuing to monitor individuals during the practice portion of each lesson.

INTERACTING WITH STUDENTS

One of the critical elements in teacher directed instruction is the interaction between teacher and students. This interaction has been the focus of many recent research efforts. Studies have shown that the way teachers interact with students can affect the students' attitudes toward school, the students' achievements, or both. Apparently simply talking with students can have a positive impact on their achievements (Stallings, 1975).

A teacher who is continually interacting with students is in touch with the students' level of comprehension. By talking, listening, and becoming more involved in monitoring student activities, teachers can assess the level of on-task behavior of the students and take immediate, brief corrective action if it drops too low. A quick question or show of hands lets the teacher know who might be having trouble with a concept and who might be ready to move on to independent practice. A teacher who is talking to students, asking them questions, and listening critically to their answers is likely to detect problems at an earlier stage than a teacher who is not interacting with students. The interacting teacher is in a much better position to monitor and tailor instruction according to the needs of the students.

Finally, the teacher who is interacting with students is likely to provide more feedback to students regarding their performances. With more feedback, students are less likely to practice errors and are more likely to continue with the learning task.

32

Because LD students need instruction that is constantly monitored and adjusted, instruction in which feedback is immediate and frequent, and instruction which is interactive, the LD teacher should organize lessons that emphasize teacher directed instruction. Unfortunately, unless teachers consciously build interactive instruction into their lesson plans LD students are not likely to receive it.

Although it is important for the LD teacher to interact with the students, not all kinds of interactions are equally valuable. Not surprisingly, interactions which are academic have been found to be more effective in facilitating student achievement than interactions that are social or managerial. The teacher who can minimize the amount of time he or she spends maintaining order, telling students where to sit, or what materials to get will have more time to tell students how to decode new words or reduce fractions.

Academic interaction may take many forms. "Teacher talk" can provide information, ask questions, or react to student performance. Each of these kinds of academic interactions appears to be useful in improving the learning of some students, at some grade levels, and on some kinds of learning tasks. There is no consensus on whether one kind of "teacher talk" should be utilized more frequently or whether there is an appropriate blend that might work best. However, several trends have been identified.

A great deal of the early research into styles of academic interactions focused on the degree of "directness" of the teacher talk. Direct talk meant giving information, lecturing, or demonstrating verbally. Less direct talk meant asking leading questions which were supposed to elicit information from the students. Some investigators in the 1960's felt that it was more advantageous for the teacher to be less direct and that interactions within the classroom should be aimed at eliciting student responses (Flanders, 1970). Flanders expected to see greater student achievement gains in classrooms where the teacher spent more time asking questions than lecturing, for example. In a number of studies which categorized teacher-student interactions in the classroom, he found that this was not necessarily the case. Flanders concluded that more direct styles of teacher-student interaction might be more appropriate when students are trying to learn factual information.

A second form of academic interaction is questioning. Questioning students serves a number of important functions. First, it is a type of drill and review for students. Second, it provides a means of overt student participation during which the teacher can be assured of the students' involvement. Third, it provides a means by which the teacher can monitor the students' understanding of the lesson.

The first studies to compare the usefulness of teacher questioning led to speculation that questioning was of greater value in classes devoted to basic skills instruction (usually earlier grades) or in classes devoted to factual learning (Flanders, 1970). Later studies have shown that the number of academic questions asked by the teacher per class period is highly linked to student achievement gains (Stallings & Kaskowitz, 1974). In one study comparing more successful teachers with less successful teachers in junior high mathematics instruction, it was found that more successful teachers asked an average of 16 more questions per class than less successful teachers (Evertson, Anderson, & Brophy, 1978).

The positive correlation between questioning and student achievement is strongest when there are straightforward answers to the questions (Brophy & Evertson, 1974). This suggests that it is most appropriate to use questioning techniques for reviewing and practicing material that has already been presented (Soar & Soar, 1973). Asking questions which students are likely to answer correctly also provides students with an opportunity for success.

A third important way in which the teacher interacts with students is by providing students with feedback on their academic performance. If students are to benefit from independent practice, they must know if their work is correct and, if not, what needs to be done to correct it. Even if students' work is correct, it is important that they receive feedback from the teacher. Feedback in general facilitates learning. It not only helps the student to whom it is directed but, in group lessons, it provides everyone with information with which to evaluate academic performance.

However, feedback and praise should not be considered synonymous terms, and the teacher must be very cautious in the use of praise with high school students. We have long been aware that praise can serve as a powerful reinforcer for students, but some researchers claim that, at the secondary school level, praise is only useful if it is used sparingly, that is, when only 5–10% of student responses are praised (Stallings, 1975). When praise is used too frequently it may no longer serve as a reinforcer.

Many special educators use praise statements spontaneously to create a warm atmosphere, to achieve a sense of equilibrium after a severe criticism to a particular student, to encourage students having difficulty, or merely as a perfunctory part of transitions ("you did a good job today") (Brophy, 1981). Care must be taken so that praise does not lose its power as a behavior modifier or reinforcer by being overused. It is prudent to tailor the use of praise to the needs of individual students in the class. Younger or more anxious students might profit from the use of praise more than older, more self-assured students. Finally, a good rule of thumb in using praise as a reinforcer for high school students is to provide only contingent praise, that is, praise which specifies the particular behavior/performance that the teacher finds praiseworthy.

STRUCTURING LESSONS

LD students do not find learning easy. To profit from instruction, they need lessons that are clearly presented, well sequenced, and well organized. Regardless of lesson content, the teacher should be concerned about the clarity of his or her explanations, the sequence of the instruction, and the organization and format of his or her teaching.

Clarity might best be described as the absence of vagueness, uncertainty, and irrelevant information in presentations. A recent study by Lana and Smith (1979) showed that lack of clarity reduces student achievement. In this study, identical lessons were presented to two matched groups of students, but in the presentation to one of the groups the teacher injected vague terms such as "sort of" and "maybe." The results showed that the explicit addition of vagueness to the lesson reduced the achievement of students in that group. Other studies have shown that when the teacher gets "off the track" by injecting irrelevant content into the lesson, students learn less. LD secondary teachers must develop clear presentations of new information and avoid vague language, digressions, and discontinuities whenever possible.

The order in which information is presented to students is also an important element in their learning (Kallison, 1980). Order may be conveyed to students by having teachers repeat key concepts as they move from one part of the lesson to the next. Or, they may follow a "rule-example-rule" sequence of presentation in which teachers state a concept, provide an elaboration of the concept, then restate the concept or rule before moving on. These approaches to presentation emphasize constant repetition of key concepts and follow a sequence which builds towards final mastery of information. There are studies that show that these techniques are related to higher student achievement (Smith & Sanders, 1981; Rosenshine, 1976).

There is some evidence that students will learn more if they are aware of the teacher's lesson structure. A number of studies in the late 1960's showed that students scored significantly higher on posttests if they were given an organizational diagram of the structure of the lesson before the lesson was presented. Kallison (1980) examined lessons in which the structure was made explicit by the teacher as the lesson progressed. The teacher would explain the organization at the beginning of the class, announce when transitions were about to occur, point out how different segments of the lessons related to one another, and provide a review at the end of the lesson. Kallison's comparisons of two lessons which were identical, except for such explicit lesson structuring by the teacher, showed a trend toward greater student gain when lesson structure was made explicit.

4 Beyond Direct Services for the Learning Disabled Adolescent

A comprehensive program for LD adolescents is likely to include more than direct instruction. For that reason, we will now discuss the indirect services that will also be part of the responsibilities of the LD teacher.

By indirect services we mean those liaison activities the LD teacher performs with regular educators who teach LD students in the mainstream. We devote less space to a discussion of indirect services than direct services but that in no way reflects our regard for their significance. Many special educators share with us the view that active, ongoing communication with regular educators is an essential part of special education services for secondary LD students. Miller and Sabatino (1978) found that LD students served by teacher consultants with no additional direct services did well, or better, in school than peers who received resource room instruction. Idol-Maestas (1983) reviewed several training programs and was encouraged by evaluation findings that suggest a positive impact of consultative services on student achievement.

Therefore, although LD teachers already contend with the heavy demands on time, energy, and ingenuity to prepare and deliver direct instruction, they should also give time and thought to the indirect service component of their jobs.

Providing indirect services is essentially a systematic communication effort. The goal of this effort is to make it easier for the LD student to meet the demands of the mainstream and graduate from high school. The key personnel with whom the LD teacher must communicate include the school administrators, the LD student's counselor, and the student's regular education teachers.

LD students often have histories of inappropriate school conduct and frequently find themselves in the principal's or vice-principal's office. They also tend to fail courses because of poor attendance (Zigmond et al., 1984). If the LD teacher makes certain that school administrators understand the LD students' problems and the LD teacher's goals for these students, the administrator may be more useful in developing cooperative plans for keeping the students in school and in compliance with school expectations. Collaboration between the LD teacher and school administrators communicates to the rest of the staff that special education is important in the eyes of the power structure within the school, and that the program's personnel and students are an integral part of the school and worthy of attention and consideration. Special educators generally need this "official" sanction in order to get cooperation from mainstream teachers.

The LD student's counselor is another key person with whom the LD teacher must communicate. In most high schools, the counselors are responsible for scheduling. The LD teacher needs to have a current copy of each student's schedule to know who the student's regular education teachers are. Through the counselor the LD teacher can monitor each student's progress in regular education classes and be alerted when a student receives poor grades.

Because the counselor is in charge of student scheduling, he or she is in a position to make decisions about the electives and vocational courses to which an LD student is assigned. In some school districts there is a prescribed program for special education students. In many others, however, beyond the basic high school requirements, the student's course of study is planned by the school counselor. Selection of courses may be a matter of expedience, with the counselor guessing what courses the student can pass, or selecting courses that meet at convenient times. Since it is important that the LD student's high school program be realistic in terms of high school graduation and post-high school adjustment, it is useful for the LD teacher to have input into the choice of courses. A good working relationship with the school counselor makes this possible.

The LD teacher will also want to have contact with all of the regular education teachers who have LD students in their classes. Through this contact, the LD teacher can coordinate the program of instruction in special education with the demands of the mainstream. Time spent with the LD teacher can be spent reinforcing skills, particularly compliance behaviors and study skills, that LD students need in their regular classes. Instruction and practice in reading comprehension, written language, mathematics, or almost any other skill can utilize materials from regular education classes.

To carry out a program of indirect services, the LD teacher can initiate formal or informal contacts with the school staff. Informal contacts are those in which the LD teacher simply makes a point of interacting with the faculty, by participating in school activities such as sponsoring a club or sharing administrative assignments such as hall duty (although in many schools special educators are exempt from administrative assignments). Some LD teachers initiate more formal communications by systematically contacting all of their students' regular education teachers, in person or by memo, so that each mainstream teacher is aware that the LD teacher is interested in the student and will support both the student and the regular education teacher in the mainstreaming effort. Another way of communicating with the regular education staff is to share with them an overview of the LD program: how the program is organized, what materials are used, what skills are taught, and what teaching techniques are employed. This can be done in a newsletter, through conversations, or by holding an "open house" periodically, during a preparation period, lunch period, before or after school, or during the "down time" of an inservice or clerical day. Regular educators are often totally unfamiliar with what a special education program is like.

Other forms of communication with the staff might be to conduct an inservice or to work intensively with a mainstream teacher to develop and implement instructional alternatives for LD students in his or her classes. These kinds of contacts are often very helpful to the regular education teachers as well as to the LD student (Laurie, Buchwach, Silverman, & Zigmond, 1978), but they are time-consuming. It may be unrealistic to expect an LD teacher to prepare inservice activities or to work in a consulting capacity with many teachers. If, however, there is administrative support for the LD program and if the teacher has established a good working relationship with the administration, release time for these tasks may be provided for the teacher. School administrators are often aware of the problems posed by the LD students in regular classes. If the LD teacher organizes a plan for implementing indirect services and presents it convincingly and professionally to the school administration, approval for the necessary release time may be forthcoming.

Whatever the format for communicating with regular educators, the major tasks of the LD teacher are to share and to collect information. Regular educators need to know about the LD program and they may need specific information about specific students. The LD teacher needs to know about the setting demands of the mainstream and about their students' performances so that they can design instruction that is appropriate and useful.

5 Recommendations for the Learning Disabilities Teacher

The task of teaching LD students at the high school level is formidable indeed. In this monograph, we have reviewed program models which have been recommended for LD adolescents. We have described planning activities which should precede the delivery of instruction. We have reviewed research which bears on the way instruction can be organized and the way students and teacher will spend class time. And we have outlined indirect, supportive services which should also be a part of a comprehensive LD program.

We see the LD teacher as a decisionmaker. In the design and delivery of instruction, the teacher has many choices. We believe that a growing body of research on effective teaching practices in mainstream education can inform the decisions that the LD practitioner has to make. We have used this research and our experiences in high schools to develop the following recommendations for the LD teacher:

1. Select several curricular components and use each to a greater or lesser extent with individual students. No single model of services for secondary LD will satisfy the needs of all LD adolescents. For a comprehensive LD program, we recommend a resource room program combined with cooperative planning and consultative services. Within the resource room setting we recommend a balanced curriculum of basic skills instruction, learning strategies, and school survival skills.

2. Conduct systematic, informal assessments at the start of each school year to help decide where to begin instruction in each curricular area to be taught in special education. Schedule frequent, direct assessments of student progress to stay informed about whether instructional objectives are being met and whether changes need to be made in a student's instructional program.

3. Remember that motivating students is an important part of the LD teacher's job. Find out what students are interested in and, to the extent possible, incorporate their interests into learning tasks. Give students reasons to keep trying by relating the current academic hurdles to goals that are attainable in the not-too-distant future. Institute both individual and group contingencies and reinforce students for active participation in the learning process.

4. Plan instruction carefully. Establish priorities so that planning time is used efficiently. Devise recordkeeping systems that are precise and that serve several purposes. Organize the physical space of the classroom so that it is neat, attractive, and supports the instructional program. Design the daily and weekly schedule to maximize the time students spend in teacher directed learning and monitored seatwork. Establish classroom management procedures so that students know what to expect and how to behave.

5. Maximize the amount of time LD students have to learn new skills. Plan lessons that reduce the amount of class time devoted to transitions, getting materials, and getting students organized. Use sound behavior-management tactics to minimize the amount of classroom time taken up with disciplinary matters. Plan more activities in which students participate overtly. Maintain a friendly yet business-like atmosphere in the classroom to discourage absenteeism.

6. Structure the classroom and daily activities so that the teacher is actively directing instruction for the maximum amount of time with the maximum number of students without compromising the goal of an individualized educational program for LD students. Plan more discussion and question-and-answer activities and fewer independent seatwork activities. Use question-and-answer times to individualize instruction. Plan for seatwork activities only when they can be monitored closely. Consider grouping for instruction not only as a means of providing more teacher directed instruction to more students but also as a means of keeping students overtly involved and on task.

7. Maximize the amount of time talking to students about academic content. Provide information in the form of lecturing, giving examples, and providing explanations. Question students a great deal. Questions should require short, factual answers which students are likely to know. Use questioning for drill and review as well as for checking the level of understanding. Always let

students know, either verbally or nonverbally, whether their answers are correct or incorrect. Praise students *sparingly* and be cautious that praise is contingent and specific. Rarely or never criticize students for poor performance.

8. Provide for clarity in lessons by eliminating irrelevant information from class discussions and reducing the level of vagueness in lesson presentations and directions.

9. Structure lessons so that they are easy for students to follow. Make certain that students can discern what is important in each lesson. Pay particular attention to sequencing of instruction. Identify the structure of the lesson at the beginning by stating the lesson objectives or by providing an anticipatory set. Or simply outline "what we are going to do today." Use transition statements. Be explicit about how one segment of the lesson relates to other segments and end lessons with a summary of what has transpired.

10. Devote at least some portion of each day to indirect services, that is, liaison work with the rest of the school faculty. Consultation with mainstream teachers and administrators is an integral part of a comprehensive program of services to the LD adolescent.

References

Adelman, H. S. (1978). The concept of intrinsic motivation: Implications for practice and research related to learning disabilities. *Learning Disability Quarterly, 1*, 43–54.

Alley, G., & Deshler, D. (1979). *Teaching the learning disabled adolescents: Strategies and methods.* Denver: Love Publishing Company.

Belcastro, F. P. (1977). *Use of behavior modification with L.D. students.* (ERIC Document Reproduction Service No. ED 135 170)

Bennett, R. E. (1982). Cautions for the use of informal measures in the educational assessment of exceptional children. *Journal of Learning Disabilities, 15*, 337–339.

Brandis, M., & Halliwell, R. (1980). *Verification of procedures to serve handicapped students: Final report—Secondary component* (Contract No. 300-79-702). Silver Spring, MD: Applied Management Sciences.

Brophy, D., & Evertson, C. (1974). *Process-product correlations in the Texas teacher effectiveness study: Final report (Research Report 74-4).* Austin: University of Texas at Austin. (ERIC Document Reproduction Service No. ED 091 094)

Brophy, J. (1981). Teacher praise: A functional analysis. *Review of Education Research, 51*(1), 5–32.

Coker, H., Lorentz, J., & Coker, J. (1976). *Interim report of Carroll County CBTC project.* Atlanta: Georgia State Department of Education.

Cooley, W. W., & Leinhardt, G. (1980). The instructional dimension study. *Educational Evaluation and Policy Analysis, 2*(1), 7–25.

Cox, J. (1980). Operation divert: A model program of learning disabled juvenile offenders. In R. H. Riegel & J. P. Mathey (Eds.), *Mainstreaming at the secondary level: Seven models that work.* Plymouth, MI: Wayne County Intermediate School District.

Cruickshank, W. M. (1977). Least-restrictive placement: Administrative wishful thinking. *Journal of Learning Disabilities, 10*(1), 5–6.

Deshler, D., Alley, G., & Carlson, S. A. (1980). Learning strategies: An approach to mainstreaming secondary students with learning disabilities. *Education Unlimited, 2*(4), 6–11.

Deshler, D., Alley, G., Warner, M. M., & Schumaker, J. B. (1981). Instructional practices for promoting skill acquisition and generalization in severely learning disabled adolescents. *Learning Disability Quarterly, 4*(4), 415–421.

Deshler, D., Lowrey, N., & Alley, G. (1979). Programming alternatives for LD adolescents: A nationwide survey. *Academic Therapy, 14,* 389–397.

Deshler, D., Schumaker, J., Lenz, B., & Ellis, E. (1984). Academic and cognitive interventions for LD adolescents: Part II. *Journal of Learning Disabilities, 17,* 170–179.

Dolly, J. P., & Pittman, B. R. (1976). *Behaviorally oriented programs for learning disabled children.* (ERIC Document Reproduction Service No. ED 117 927).

Egner, A. (1974). *The challenge of special education in regular high school classrooms: Applications of the behavioral model.* (ERIC Document Reproduction Service No. 102 790)

Evans, S. (1980). The consultant role of the resource teacher. *Exceptional Children, 46,* 402–404.

Evertson, C., Anderson, L., & Brophy, J. (1978). *Texas Junior High School Study: Final report on process-outcome relationships* (Report No. 406). Austin: University of Texas, Research Development Center for Teacher Education.

Flanders, J. (1970). *Analyzing teacher behavior.* Reading, MA: Addison Wesley.

Fuchs, L. S., & Fuchs, D. (1984). Criterion-referenced assessment without measurement: How accurate for special education? *Remedial and Special Education, 5,* 29–32.

Good, T., & Brophy, J. (in press). Teacher behavior and student achievement. In M. C. Wittrack (Ed.), *Handbook of research on teaching* (3rd Edition). New York: Macmillan.

Goodman, L., & Mann, L. (1976). *Learning disabilities in the secondary schools: Issues and practices.* New York: Grune & Stratton.

Hartwell, J. D., Wiseman, D. E., & Van Reusen, A. V. (1979). Modifying course content for mildly handicapped students at the secondary level. *TEACHING Exceptional Children, 12,* 28–32.

Hunter, M. (1974). The science of the art of teaching. In D. Allen & J. Hecht (Eds.), *Controversy in education.* Philadelphia: W. B. Saunders.

Hunter, M. (1978, March). *A clinical theory of instruction.* Paper presented at Teacher Effectiveness Workshop, University of California, Los Angeles.

Idol-Maestas, L. (1983). *Special educator's consultation handbook.* Rockville, MD: Aspen Systems Corporation.

IMPRESS training manual. (Vol. V-F, Part I.) (1984). Tallahassee, FL: FDLRS Clearinghouse Information Center, Department of Education, Bureau of Education for Exceptional Students.

Kallison, J. (1980). *Organization of the lesson as it affects student achievement.* Unpublished doctoral dissertation, University of Texas, Austin.

Keller, H. R. (1983). Assessment. In C. R. Smith (Ed.), *Learning disabilities: The interaction of learner, task, and setting.* Boston: Kluiver-Nijhoff.

Kerr, M. M., & Nelson, C. M. (1983). *Strategies for managing behavior problems in the classroom.* Columbus, OH: Charles E. Merrill.

Knight, M. F., Meyers, H. W., Paolucci-Whitcomb, P., Hasazi, S. E., & Nevin, A. (1981). A four-year evaluation of consulting teacher service. *Behavioral Disorders, 6,* 92–100.

Kohnke, R., Zigmond, N., & Miller, S. (1985). *Assessing the impact of teacher inservice on secondary special education classrooms with observational measures: Preliminary findings from the first two years.* Abstract submitted to American Education Research Association for presentation at San Francisco.

Lana, M., & Smith, L. (1979). The effect of low inference teacher clarity inhibitors on student achievement. *Journal of Teacher Education, 31*, 55–57.

Laurie, T., Buchwach, L., Silverman, R., & Zigmond, N. (1978). Teaching secondary learning disabled students in the mainstream. *Learning Disability Quarterly, 1*, 62–72.

Leinhardt, G. (1977). Program evaluation: An empirical study of individualized instruction. *American Education Research Journal, 14*, 277–293.

Leinhardt, G., Hammond, K., Weidman, C., & Figura, C. (1984, April). *Introduction and integration of classroom routines by expert teachers.* Paper presented at the American Educational Research Association, New Orleans, Louisiana.

Lerner, J. W. (1976). *Children with learning disabilities: Theories, diagnosis, teaching strategies.* Boston: Houghton Mifflin.

Lilly, M. S., & Givens-Ogle, L. D. (1981). Teacher consultation: Present, past, and future. *Behavioral Disorders, 6*, 73–77.

Long, J. D., & Frye, V. H. (1977). *Making it till Friday.* Princeton, NJ: Princeton Book Company.

Mann, L., Goodman, L., & Wiederholt, J. (1978). *Teaching the learning disabled adolescent.* Boston: Houghton Mifflin.

Marsh, G. E., Gearheart, C. K., & Gearheart, B. R. (1978). *The learning disabled adolescent.* St. Louis: C. V. Mosby.

McGlothlin, J. E. (1981). The school consultation committee: An approach to implementing a teacher consultation model. *Behavioral Disorders, 6*, 101–107.

Meyen, E. L., & Lehr, D. (1980). Evolving practices in assessment and in intervention: The case for intensive instruction. *Exceptional Quarterly, 1*(2), 19–26.

Miller, T. L., & Davis, E. E. (1982). *The mildly handicapped student.* New York: Grune & Stratton.

Miller, T. L., & Sabatino, D. A. (1978). An evaluation of the teacher consultation model as an approach to mainstreaming. *Exceptional Children, 45*, 86–91.

Mirkin, P. K., Fuchs, L. S., & Deno, S. L. (Eds.). (1982). *Considerations for designing a continuous evaluation system: An integrative review.* (Monograph #20). Minneapolis: University of Minnesota, Institute for Research of Learning Disabilities.

Morrissey, P. A., & Semmel, M. I. (1976). Instructional models for the learning disabled. *Theory into Practice, 14*, 110–122.

Mosby, R. (1980). The application of the developmental by-pass procedure to LD adolescents. *Journal of Learning Disabilities, 13*(7), 21–27.

Needels, M., & Stallings, J. (1975). *Classroom processes related to absence rate.* Menlo Park, CA: Stanford Research Institute.

Pittsburgh Public Schools. (1985). *Guide to effective teaching strategies.* Pittsburgh, PA: Author.

Riegel, R. H. (1980). The model resource room project. In R. H. Riegel & J. P. Mathoy (Eds.), *Mainstreaming at the secondary level: Seven models that work*. Plymouth, MI: Wayne County Intermediate School District.

Rosenshine, B. (1976). Classroom instruction. In N. L. Gage (Ed.), *The psychology of teaching methods: The seventy-fifth yearbook of the National Society for the Study of Education* (pp. 335–371). Chicago: University of Chicago Press.

Ryor, J. (1978). 94–142: The perspective of regular education. *Learning Disability Quarterly, 1*(2), 6–14.

Sabatino, D. A., Sabatino, A. C., & Mann, L. (1983). *Discipline and behavioral management*. Rockville, MD: Aspen Systems Corporation.

Sear, R. (1973). *Follow through classroom process management and pupil growth (1970–71)*. Final Report. Gainesville, FL: University of Florida, College of Education.

Sheldon, J., Sherman, J. A., Hazel, J. S., Meyen, E. L., & Schumaker, J. B. (1982). *Developing a social skills curriculum for mildly handicapped adolescents and young adults: Some problems and approaches*. (Research Monograph No. 11). Lawrence, KS: The University of Kansas Institute for Research in Learning Disabilities.

Silverman, R., Zigmond, N., & Sansone, J. (1981). Teaching coping skills to adolescents with learning problems. *Focus on Exceptional Children, 13*, 1–20.

Smith, C. R. (1983). *Learning disabilities: The interaction of learner, task, and setting*. Boston: Little, Brown, & Company.

Smith, L., & Sanders, K. (1981). The effects on student achievement and student perception of varying structure in social studies content. *Journal of Education Research, 74*, 333–336.

Smith-Davis, J., Burke, P. J., & Noel, M. M. (1984). *Personnel to educate the handicapped in America: Supply and demand from a programmatic viewpoint*. College Park, MD: University of Maryland, Institute for the Study of Exceptional Children and Youth.

Soar, R. S., & Soar, R. M. (1973). *Classroom behavior, pupil characteristics and pupil growth for the school year and the summer*. Gainesville, FL: University of Florida, Institute for Development of Human Resources.

Stallings, J. (1975). Implementation and child effects of teaching practices in follow through classrooms. *Monographs of the Society for Research in Child Development, 40*(7–8).

Stallings, J. (1980a). Allocated academic learning time revisited, or beyond time on task. *Education Researcher, 8*, 11–16.

Stallings, J. (1980b). *How to change the process of teaching basic reading skills in secondary schools*. Phase II & III. Final Report. Menlo Park, CA: SRI International. (ERIC Document Reproduction Service No. ED 210 671)

Stallings, J. (1981). *What research has to say to administrators of secondary schools about effective teaching and staff development*. Menlo Park, CA: Stanford Research Institute. (ERIC Document Reproduction Service No. ED 209 748)

Stallings, J., & Kaskowitz, D. (1974). *Follow through classroom observation evaluation 1972–1973*. Menlo Park, CA: Stanford Research Institute.

Torgesen, J. K. (1982). The learning disabled child as an inactive learner: Education implications. *Topics in Learning and Learning Disabilities, 2*, 45–52.

Utley, B. L. (1982). *The effects of various forms of data on the ability to analyze trends in student performance.* Unpublished doctoral dissertation, University of Pittsburgh, Pittsburgh.

Weiderholt, J. L., & McEntire, B. (1980). Educational options for handicapped adolescents. *Exceptional Education Quarterly, 1*(2), 1–10.

Wiseman, D. E. (1981). The nonreading parallel curriculum. *Academic Therapy, 20*(2), 14–20.

Zigmond, N. (1978). A prototype of comprehensive services for secondary students with learning disabilities: A preliminary report. *Learning Disability Quarterly, 1,* 39–49.

Zigmond, N. (1984). *Annual report: Teacher center project, handicapped personnel preparation.* Washington, DC: Special Education Programs, Education Department.

Zigmond, N., Brownlee, J., Laurie, T., & Stanek, S. (1981). *Mainstreaming in elementary schools: A guide for inservice programs for elementary educators.* Pittsburgh, PA: University of Pittsburgh, Special Education Department.

Zigmond, N., Kerr, M. M., Brown, G., & Harris, A. (1984, April). *School survival skills in secondary school age special education students.* Paper presented at American Educational Research Association, New Orleans.

Zigmond, N., Levin, E., & Laurie, T. (1985). Managing the mainstream: An analysis of teacher attitudes and student performance in mainstream high school programs. *Journal of Learning Disabilities, 18,* 505–568.

Zigmond, N., Vallecorsa, A., & Silverman, R. (1983). *Assessment for instructional planning in special education.* Englewood Cliffs, NJ: Prentice-Hall.